DEPRESSION . . . .
THE WAY OUT

DEPRESSION....
THE WAY OUT

DON SPARKES

CHRISTIAN LITERATURE CRUSADE

CHRISTIAN LITERATURE CRUSADE
51 The Dean, Alresford, Hants. SO24 9BJ

U.S.A.
P.O. Box 1449, Fort Washington,
Pennsylvania 19034.

AUSTRALIA
Box 91, Pennant Hills, N.S.W. 2120.

NEW ZEALAND
P.O. Box 976 Auckland, C.I.

also in

Europe, Canada,
Central America, South America,
West Indies, Africa, India,
Indonesia, Far East

© 1972

Christian Literature Crusade

First published 1965

Revised edition 1972

New edition 1991

ISBN 0-900284-31-5

Cover designed by Design for Print, Eastbourne.
Printed in England by Design for Print, Eastbourne.

THE NATURE OF DEPRESSION

"Depression is hell"

This is the way Bernard described the harrowing experience from which he had just emerged. A few months before he had been a radiant Christian, witnessing to his fellow steelworkers. He had come to our church to speak on *My Faith and My Job,* and had thrilled the congregation with his radiant sincerity. Within a matter of days all this had gone. Instead of joy there was now worry, darkness, and boredom. He could not read or concentrate on anything worthwhile. The darkness became so intense that he began to feel the only way out was to take his life. *Hell* was the only term he could use.

One reason for this was the fact that God was, so it seemed, no longer a part of Bernard's experience. Had God withdrawn Himself? Men do put themselves sometimes beyond the love of God by outwardly rejecting and spurning their Creator, but we only know of one person from whom God has ever deliberately withdrawn Himself, and that person was His Son, Jesus Christ. This withdrawal was only for a moment, and was due to Christ bearing the sin of the world. His cry "My God, my God, why hast thou forsaken me?" (Mark 15.34) gives us a glimpse of the depression of soul through which our Lord was going. C. H. Spurgeon, the great preacher of the last century, when preaching on these words of Christ, said something rather like Bernard:

> "A man may bear depression of spirit about worldly matters if he feels he has God to go to. He is cast down but not in despair. Like David he dialogues with himself and he enquires, 'Why art thou cast down, O my soul? and why art thou disquieted in me? hope thou in God: for I shall yet praise him . . .' But if the Lord be once withdrawn, if the comfortable light of His presence be shadowed, even for an hour, there is torment within the heart, which I can only liken to the prelude of hell."

Bernard found that his depression was not just a personal thing. It affected others. His home became an unhappy place not just for him but for his wife and children. It was like a disease, it spread to and affected those with whom he came into contact. Depression was just as infectious as his former joy. Those who have got out on the wrong side of the bed will know a little of the way a mood can affect the others in the house and at work. How miserable it is to work with those who always have the Monday-morning feeling! The person who, as one writer put it: "Not only do they have cellars in their emotional houses, as everybody does, but they live in them."

Very often depression is a normal reaction to an abnormal situation. We see this in the large percentage of people attending doctors' surgeries, people who have reacted to unforeseen changes in circumstances by becoming anxiety-prone or neurotic. When we look into the reasons for Bernard's illness we find it was his reaction to something new to his experience. In his case depression had physical, mental, and spiritual reasons all springing from the basic change in his life when he found himself off work and idle for the first time in his life.

My aim in this booklet is to try and deal with spiritual depression. Before I do this a brief note on depression springing from physical or mental causes is included. Anyone who believes himself to be suffering from severe depression of any kind should, of course, consult his doctor.

Part of the trouble may be physical

Bergsten, in his book *Pastoral Psychology**, writes:
"Many physical diseases, and many conditions of bodily disorder, especially in the endocrine system, are accompanied by characteristic mental and emotional changes. Very often these take the form of depression which may rise to the intensity of anguish or despair. A person who is assailed by thoughts and feelings of this kind seldom realises that they are of physical origin."

Bernard had developed an acute ear trouble. Because of this he became susceptible to giddiness, which made it dangerous for him to be near machinery. He was also in his middle years when

---

* G. Bergsten : *Pastoral Psychology* (George Allen & Unwin, 1951).

hormonal changes in the body, relating in some way to the change of life in women, were taking place. For him the cure of his depression was related in a very real way with the cure of his ear complaint. Not until this was well on the way to being dealt with did the depressive state abate. Some physical reasons for depression can be dealt with easily enough, and with little enough effort, and the earlier we go and talk with our doctor, the sooner we shall receive the advice we need. As a famous London preacher once wisely said:

> "It is a religious tragedy if you are depressed and irritable, and affecting others with depression and bad temper, when as much Kruschen's as would go on a sixpence could renew your faith in God and man."

Some other physical causes are not so easy to deal with. Often the first need is that the cause of depression should be seen for what it is, and made the best of. An adolescent, or a woman in the change of life, or a man in his late forties, all experience hormonal changes in the body; the pregnant woman whose baby is lying low down in the womb, or the mother of a few days recovering from the shock of birth and readjustments in her hormones – such folk cannot do much but accept the situation. The changes in the body will soon pass and the depression will go, and the grateful realisation of this fact frequently is all that is needed.

Yet other physical upsets, affecting the soul with gloom, may be warning of serious disorder in the body and if this is the case no delay should be allowed before we see our doctor. In some cases, the earlier he can diagnose and treat us the better will be the possibility of cure.

The fact that body and soul react on each other is a truth we all recognise. This is one very good reason for taking care of our bodies – taking enough exercise, adequate sleep, eating the right kind of food, not misusing the body in any way. We should strive to make our bodies fit, clean, and beautiful. Then we can pray with the hymnwriter:

> Breathe on me, Breath of God,
> Till I am wholly Thine,
> Until this earthly part of me,
> Glows with Thy fire divine.

Part of the trouble may be mental

Bernard had always been a very active person. He loved his work. His spare time since his conversion was taken up with service to the community. His life was so organised that there was no time to be idle, to sit and think.

Now he was off work. Weeks, maybe months, would have to be spent idle. His giddiness made it impossible to read or do anything. **The reaction to this abnormal situation was normal** – he became depressed, miserable, and irritable. No one seemed to be able to help him. Each day took him further into the mire until he felt the only way out was to end it all by suicide – never an answer anyone should contemplate!

Boredom is only one of the many mental causes for depression. The most common one occurs in hypersensitive persons – the people who drive themselves hard, who have ideals which they must live up to, who are over-conscientious, and who feel guilty if they relax. Failing to live up to their ideals they fall into deep depression over their failures. Such folk would begin to find a cure if they could be helped to take life less seriously. We cannot be but what we are and must advance a step at a time instead of trying to be now what it will take a lifetime to become.

Overwork and overstrain saps our very lifeblood, and it is not surprising to find Christians having bouts of depression if they take too much on, or ignore the need for a holiday and change. In such cases when one is mentally exhausted it is worth-while sitting down and considering seriously dropping this or that commitment, and working out how one can get away from it all, if only for a weekend.

Some are depressed because they are never appreciated. They try to do their best, yet those working or living with them just never see what they do. All is accepted with never a word of praise or thanks. How many yearn to be appreciated and are downcast and depressed because the words of thanks and praise never come. Praise is better than any tonic. A bouquet for the living is worth ten wreaths for the dead. If we Christians could get into the habit of looking round for things to praise instead of complain or grouse about we would banish depression for many people. Try it with your own minister at church when something has been said which has helped you, try it in the shops when you have been helped to find what you want by the assistant, try it when you sit down to the next meal at home!

I remember reading about an interesting experiment with babies. A film record was made of changes of expression on a baby's face during periods of absence from its mother. It was found that if the mother was absent too long when the baby was needing her it went through phases of what the author called "profound depression" – that is, it appeared to experience something not unlike what an adult would know. If this is so, it seems most unwise continually to leave a child to cry itself to sleep, as one school of thought advocated, for some depressions may well be related to the childhood experience of being left alone. This may throw light on the fact that some live in dread of losing someone they love, and an actual loss brings this profound depression surging back into consciousness.

So often we point to things outside ourselves that have brought about worry and depression yet the trouble is within us. It is how we face situations which matter, whether we have our lives based on the solid foundation of Christ or everything just resting on the sands of changing feelings – as in the story of the two houses which Jesus used so pointedly in His Sermon on the Mount. If all is well within, then we can cope with any situation outside ourselves, even if it is a serious physical disability which could overwhelm the soul with darkness. I have seen Christians overcome depressing illnesses such as diabetes and sclerosis because of the inner joy they had from contact with Christ. As Bergsten says:

> "A deep spring of inward happiness refuses to
> be dammed up, and from time to time it breaks

through and manifests itself despite the adverse physical (*and I would add, mental*) state against which it must contend."[*]

Christianity, remember, is "good news" – that is, good news for every situation which a man or woman may find themselves in. That Christ can deal with the situation is a basic Christian truth, but He may choose to use a Christian psychiatrist to help us to find wholeness of mind just as He may use the doctor in bringing about wholeness of body.

Part of the trouble may be spiritual

It would be nothing more than a quick look at the physical and mental causes if Bernard's trouble cleared up when his ear got better or when his boredom ended with his return to activity. But his depression was something deeper – it reached down to the very spiritual depths of his being. For him as a Christian it was the spiritual havoc that had been wrought that concerned him most. God seemed to be no longer present. Vital prayer was now a thing of the past, and no longer a present joyful experience. He could pray, but somehow did not seem to be in contact with the Lord. The reading of God's Word was no longer a joy to him. He had lost his hunger for the things of God – somehow the Bible did not seem relevant.

The trouble was that Bernard was somehow blaming the Lord for this state. He went to bed at night resenting the Lord's dealings with him. He ignored St. Paul's wisdom: ". . . never let the sun set

[*] G. Bergsten: *Pastoral Psychology.*

upon your *exasperation*" – as Moffatt translated Eph. 4:26; he thus awoke in the morning with his resentment and depression and irritability even more a part of him. How he needed to come to the Lord seeking forgiveness, a new start, new life in the Spirit and power to live victoriously. Yet he did not seem able to do this. Then one afternoon he sat in his home thinking. The house was quiet with the children at school, and he was turning over in his mind some words which a workmate had said only that morning:

"Your faith must make quite a difference to you in the situation you find yourself in!"

"Why is this not true?" he thought. "Why as a Christian am I in such a state as this? He is right. My faith should make a difference."

He opened his Bible and read at random till he came to a verse that he knew by heart. This time its relevance came alive for him – the words of Jesus in Matthew's Gospel: "Come to me, all who labour and are heavy laden, and I will give you rest" (Matt. 11:28 RSV).

Why he had not come to Jesus before with his burden and trouble he was not quite sure, but there was no time like the present. So he poured out his heart to the Lord – shared the situation with Him. This, as he said afterwards, ". . . lifted the fog and brought me into the glorious sunshine of His presence again." He brought his burden to Jesus and left it there instead of taking it up again on his own shoulders.

In Bernard's case this led to a striking change. The depression which had sprung from, and reacted back on, his whole being, was now cast out. *He was free to be recommissioned for service.*

While not recommending this dangerous and chancy way of opening the Bible at random for a message from God, this incident well illustrates the danger of flouting spiritual laws. We recognise readily enough that if we overwork and allow ourselves to be ridden by worry then there is a possibility of a nervous breakdown. The same is true of overworking the body or misusing it. We must take sufficient food and rest to function properly. Bernard will tell you that his spiritual trouble resulted partly from neglect of the means of grace; he especially mentions the missing of his morning time of prayer and Bible-reading. It was dangerous, for it meant that when his faith was needed to combat the depression coming from his physical and mental states it was so weak that for a time it was useless. He knew the answer was in the Lord, yet somehow could not get to Him.

How necessary it is, in fact how *more* necessary it is, to keep our daily times of prayer and Bible-reading, our meditation and our meeting with other Christians for worship and fellowship, when things are difficult and life becomes a struggle. It is not without reason that Thomas doubted the Resurrection of the Lord considering he was not found in fellowship with the other disciples when the Lord appeared among them.

2

THE EXAMPLE OF ELIJAH

In this second part we turn to a classic example of
spiritual depression as recorded by the writer of the
sacred record of 1 Kings 19. As we look through
this we will find comfort in the fact that even the
great men of God know what it is to be depressed.
We shall see what contributed to Elijah's condition
and the steps God took to bring healing to his
servant. Two of the great things about the Bible
are that as we read its pages we see ourselves re-
flected, and the Holy Spirit shows us the answer to
our own need – two good reasons for taking time
each day to read some part of the Bible.

Elijah is a man of God, in fact *the* man of God for
that moment in the history of the world. It was
Elijah who saved the worship of God from being
obliterated. It was Elijah who began the prophetic
ministry that would finally purify and preserve the
religion of the Jewish people, making it ready for
the coming of Jesus Christ to fulfil the hopes and
longings of the Old Testament, and complete the
Revelation of God to men.

When Elijah appeared on the scene Israel, the
northern kingdom of the Jews, was in a most
critical position. Ahab was on the throne, a man

who had married a Sidonian named Jezebel. This woman was a very strong personality and dominated and organised her husband and the affairs of the nation. She was not content, as were the wives of Solomon a hundred years before, just to have a temple dedicated to the god of her homeland. Jezebel could not tolerate Melkart, the Baal god of Sidon she worshipped, being less than on an equal footing with Jehovah, the God of the Israelites. She therefore imported priests and prophets from Sidon to establish and propagate the Sidonian religion on a national scale. But this did not content her. Having got so far, she decided that the worship to Jehovah must go. So she murdered many of the priests and prophets of Jehovah – and Ahab, the supposed leader of the nation's religion, did not raise a finger of protest.

If something was not done soon the worship of Jehovah would be gone. It is at this moment that Elijah appears. He proclaims God's judgement to the king, and then after this judgement of severe drought has run its course, demands a showdown between the two rival religions. All the people are gathered on Mount Carmel and the people are challenged to choose, once and for all, the God they will serve. The God who consumes the prepared sacrifice by fire is the true God. Then follows one of the most dramatic passages in the Bible: Elijah standing alone, jeering at the prophets of Baal, rebuilding the broken altar of Jehovah, calling down fire from heaven, killing (and thus stamping out a national religion) the prophets and priests of Baal. Then he prays successfully for rain on the scorched land, and runs eighteen miles ahead of the returning king to Jezreel, the town where the king had his palace.

It is at this point we reach the chapter where Elijah is seen as a broken man. He is on the run from the enraged Jezebel. He comes to the point of despair, praying for death to take him. What a transformation in a man who had a little while before stood against the whole nation, a man who had through his great courage and faith restored the worship of the God of their fathers to the people of of Israel! How can we understand this depression? What has brought him so low so quickly?

The experience of Mount Carmel had obviously called upon everything that he had. His lifeblood had been almost drained dry in the conflict. Emotionally he had spent himself completely, so that when a threatening letter from Jezebel was received he was too deflated to stand up against the incensed queen. To ignore the woman he had never before shown any fear of was now beyond him. The only thing he felt he could do was to run for his life. In his running away he got to the point where he was too depressed even to have a companion. We read that when he got to the wilderness in the southern part of Judah he left his servant and went on alone. He was now too low in spirits even to talk to anyone. Soon he finds a juniper tree and lies down under it. Exhausted, wrapped in gloom, he prays for death in words which probably many a depressed person has felt like using: "It is enough; now, O Lord, take away

my life; for I am no better than my fathers"
(1 Kings 19:4 RSV).

In a sense it is not so surprising that he is in this
state considering all that he has gone through. He
thought most probably that his work was now over
and he could look on as a religious revival swept the
country. Instead he is threatened with his life. **His
reaction in the face of this abnormal situation
is normal** when we take into account his exhausted
condition. We would have been in the same state,
no doubt.

This is one of the dangers of living on one's
nerves or having a religion that is too exciting. One
is left emotionally and mentally deflated and unable
to cope with the new situations in life that arise.

St. John of the Cross calls one type of religious
depression "the dark night of the soul". It is a
period of deep depression which usually follows
hard on the heels of a very strong sense of the
Divine Presence. A state of spiritual drought is
experienced when no help is received from prayer
or meditation or any other of the means of grace.
God seems to be far away; no longer can the soul
enjoy real communion with Him: "The soul has
entered a dark silent place from which even God
seems absent."

It has been observed that this sort of depression –
the sort through which Elijah was now going – is
usually a transition period when one is moving into
a yet higher knowledge and experience of God.
This is what Elijah was to know, yet for the moment
all that was real to him was the darkness. All he
now longed for was death.

18

What a comfort to know that no one is immune from depression! Even the greatest of saints have gone through this dark valley of the shadow. Yet it is often the valley that leads through to "the house of the Lord" – the presence of God. Sometimes, as the shepherds pasturing their sheep along the Jericho road know, the journey through "the valley of the shadow of death" is the only way to new pasture land.

We now turn from the depression of Elijah to the way of deliverance made possible by the Lord's dealing with him – the cure as prescribed by the Divine Physician. Maybe you will find a similar cure as you note how another was healed.

God shields His servant

A desert is not the place to lie down and give up – as many have found to their cost! The wilderness was semi-desert and no place for a man to be alone with no provision made for his journey. Hunger, thirst, exposure to the day's heat and the night's cold, these would soon make the prayer of Elijah one answered in the affirmative.

God has more work for Elijah to do. It is not yet time for him to lay down his life or his task. We read that the Lord sent an angel to look after him and to protect him while he slept and to provide for him when he awoke. In this way God brought home to his servant the fact that he was greatly loved and that his life was still very useful, two facts Elijah desperately needed to be reminded of.

To a person who is spiritually depressed the first stage of restoration is to remember the way God has met one's needs, and how he gives us so much in life to enjoy. I remember one person who had been confined to a chair for a number of years, saying how wonderful life was to her. She told me how she looked forward to the springtime so that she could see the tree outside her window breaking into new leaf, the flowers in her garden showing their faces to the sun, the birds beginning to build their nests again. So many things that I, with full health, had missed. It is this sensing of the goodness of God, revealed in the good things He daily pours upon us, that will help to banish the depression, especially when we recall that God gives to us who are so ungrateful; He protects us who so often forget Him. A knowledge of all the Lord is doing for us can only fill us with gratitude. A sense of gratitude is something with light in it, something which cannot but help to banish the darkness within us.

"Count your blessings," as the old hymn says, "Name them one by one, and it will surprise you what the Lord has done." If we really did this each day, depression of this kind for many would be an unknown experience.

God shares his burden

Strengthened with food supernaturally supplied, Elijah wanders in the wilderness for forty days – one day for every year that disobedient Israel had wandered in the desert when Moses was leading them from Egypt to the Promised Land. Elijah was making for Mount Horeb, the mountain where Moses had met with God and had received the Ten

Commandments. Maybe Elijah hoped that if he could once again stand on this ground made sacred by the Presence of God, he would once again find himself in communion with the One he felt separated from. The "dark night of the soul" would be over, a new experience of the Divine Presence would be his.

He was not disappointed. Once arrived at Horeb and lodging in a cave, "the word of the Lord came to him" (1 Kings 19:9 RSV). Whether this was an appearance of Christ in His pre-incarnate state, or whether it was God speaking to the quiet of his heart in that still, awesome place, we do not know. But what we do know is important, for it is the second necessary step in dealing with the depressive state of the man of God.

The Lord asks a question: "What are you doing here, Elijah?" The question was so framed that Elijah had the opportunity he needed to unburden himself, to share his feeling, his resentments, his gloom, with someone who could understand him.

All the poison of his soul is emptied out. Like Christian at the cross, in Bunyan's *Pilgrim's Progress*, the burden that he had been carrying, the burden that had been breaking him, rolled off his back. Once he had unburdened himself he could stand up straight again. He was that bit nearer to being usable again.

> "I have been very jealous for the Lord God of hosts: for the children of Israel have forsaken thy covenant, thrown down thine altars, and slain thy prophets with the sword; and I, even

I only, am left; and they seek my life, to take it away" (I Kings 19:10).

It is a sad story that Elijah tells to the Lord, yet now it is shared – it is being carried by another. It can never be Elijah's and only Elijah's burden any more. The work of the Christian minister and the modern psychiatrist is therefore anticipated by God Himself.

Those who are depressed and bowed down nearly always have a grievance, a problem, a difficulty. This is their reaction to an abnormal situation and their depression cannot be overcome alone. It is therefore very important that it is shared. Find a friend who understands you, or maybe the minister of your church if he is one with whom you can talk. Give up what is on your mind. It will be an easier burden to bear once it is shared with another.

So many will see this need and will share their burden with someone, but will not go on to share it with the Lord. He has made us, so naturally He understands us better than anyone else can do. St. Peter says, "Cast all your anxieties on him, for he cares about you" (I Pet. 5:7 RSV). You can do just what Elijah did – share your burden with the Lord. Tell Him how you feel, be honest with Him, replace your polite prayers with honesty. Tell Him of your grievances. Put Him into the picture about the situation you are finding it so impossible to face. We can do this because He "cares" for us – and cares so much that He is willing to take the load from our shoulders – we can "cast" it on Him.

God shows Himself

The next thing Elijah needed was a new revelation of God, and this is just what the Lord intended to give him! He is told to go out of the cave and stand on the mount "before the Lord". Obediently Elijah responds, and through his obedience he entered into a new conception of the Lord and His ways.

In this theophany a great wind blew, breaking the rocks; then came an earthquake, and then a fire. It must have seemed to Elijah as if the whole mountain was erupting around him. Each phase of the theophany had the same message – "the Lord was not in" the wind, earthquake, or fire. But He *was* in the "still small voice". It was when this sound was heard that Elijah wrapped his face in his mantle, hiding himself so that he did not look upon the awesome God. The new revelation would mean one thing to Elijah. No more would God speak to man by a violent fire from heaven; in future it would be by the quiet words of mercy and love. Elijah the fiery prophet of God would give way to the new type of ministry to men's hearts and lives, the ministry that would be exerted by the prophet's successor Elisha, and later by Jesus Himself.

There is nothing like a new revelation of God for dealing with depression. The mystics have found that "the dark night of the soul" is often a prelude to such a thing. If this proves to be so, then the depression was well worth going through.

A new revelation is needed by so many. For many Christians their experience of God is a round of busy-ness in His service, hurried prayers, emotional uplift at the big meeting, listening to one speaker after another. It is all noise and activity. No wonder we become empty, finished, and drained dry!

We may need to learn with Elijah that God is in the stillness. He will speak to us in a way that will lead us to open our lives to His healing Spirit and give us a deep desire to be filled completely by the same Holy Spirit. We need to sit quietly and meditate on some attribute of God until the wonder of His love or His truth sinks deep into our souls. In that stillness will come a new conception of God. Into our hearts will come a new Spirit-filled peace and joy that begins to banish the fog encircling our depressed personality.

The American-born poet John Greenleaf Whittier, as a Quaker, knew more about this kind of Divine Presence than many Christians in the other denominations which have overlooked to some extent the importance of silent meditation. He reminds us, in one of the loveliest hymns in our hymnbooks, of the hills:

> Where Jesus knelt to share with Thee
> The silence of eternity,
> Interpreted by love!

In the same hymn, Whittier refers, very meaningfully, to the passage we are studying:

> Breathe through the heats of our desire
> Thy coolness and Thy balm;
> Let sense be dumb, let flesh retire;
> Speak through the earthquake, wind, and fire,
> O still small voice of calm!

Let us give God the chance so to reveal Himself to us.

God shatters self-centredness

We are not only told about the still small voice, but we are told what the voice said. Elijah is asked the second time, "What are you doing here?" The purpose of the question this time is to find out whether the prophet still felt he was on his own, and whether he was still as self-centred as before. Yes, he was still the same – exactly the same answer is given. This is surprising in view of the new revelation that he had come into.

It is essential for Elijah that this self-centredness is dealt with, for the castle of self was becoming a fortress into which he was retreating. Look how dominant the self has become: "I have been jealous for the Lord . . . I, even I only, am left; and they seek my life, to take it away . . ." Elijah was the only one true to the Lord, so he thought; everyone else had forsaken Him.

It is amazing that such a man of God should indulge in such a self-centred bit of reasoning, yet he passionately believed what he said, and because of this he felt tremendously lonely.

The Lord shatters self-centredness by telling His servant that he was not the only true worshipper of Jehovah left. Far from it – at least seven thousand others in Israel had not bowed the knee to Baal. Things were not so bad as appeared from the depressive angle. God's faithful ones are sometimes God's hidden ones.

When I have felt this type of depression I have found it is my own self-centredness that has been the trouble. There have been times when, like Elijah, I have felt myself to be the only one doing

God's will, while the rest in the church have been going after the things of the world!

There is a chance that what you are going through springs from self-centredness or self-pity. It is not easy to see ourselves as we really are. It takes courage and honesty to look within. If *self* proves to be the cause of the trouble, then the Lord will have to deal with it; for not until the glasshouse we have built round ourselves is shattered can the cool refreshing breeze of God's love reach us.

We must be freed from the self that cuts us off from others, that makes us feel so alone. For the Christian it must no longer be self "but Christ". As Paul said – and do not rest until the truth of these words becomes real in your life –

> "I have been crucified with Christ; it is no longer I who live, but Christ who lives in me; and the life I now live in the flesh I live by faith in the Son of God, who loved me and gave himself for me" (Gal. 2:20 RSV).

God shapes his future

Elijah is now given some new work to do. He was not left either in his depression or in the wilderness. If he had not been recommissioned the cure would have been incomplete.

The prophet is given three tasks. Two were to do with judgement, the third with love. Jehu and Hazael were to be anointed as kings – kings who could bring the judgement of God on a rebellious Israel. More important, perhaps, is the commission to anoint Elisha as a prophetic successor to Elijah.

This would mean that the fiery ministry which saved the situation in Jezebel's day was now to give way to the quiet ministry of love and mercy. God was to speak to His people with the still, small voice of loving concern.

On his going from Horeb to carry out the Lord's commands the cure, like that of the lepers in the Gospel story, was complete. When we meet Elijah again there is no sign of discouragement or depression. Instead he is as active and vigorous on God's behalf as ever he was before. By the time Elisha takes over from Elijah the religion of Jehovah is enjoying the revival that had begun on Mount Carmel – for that day had really been the turning point in the history of Israel.

*   *   *

Like Elijah, our steelworker, Bernard, whose story we were tracing in the first part of this booklet, found that his complete cure was when he was re-commissioned for service. When he found himself physically and mentally on his feet, and once again rejoicing in renewed contact with the Lord, he was given a new piece of service. It was something that would take him completely out of himself. He could lose himself in service to others in need.

This is possibly a test for some suffering from spiritual depression: whether or not we really *want* to be restored. Are we prepared to lose our life in service to others in order to find out? Such a readiness could mean nothing less than being recommissioned. As we joyfully turn our faces to new tasks, we will step out of our little world right into involvement in the needs of the larger world outside. Instead of a depression cutting us off from others there will be an expression of God's concern for others.

* * *

In our experience of being lifted out of the mire of depression on to the sure ground of serving the Lord, the Holy Spirit has been at work. He has dealt with us right to the depths of our own subconscious. He brings not only healing but joy.

The way forward now is to avoid what Paul calls "quenching the Spirit" (1 Thess. 5:19). If you look at the context of this verse you will see the way to keep the fire of the Spirit burning brightly in your life. It is to keep rejoicing at all times, never to get out of the habit of prayer, thanking and praising the Lord in all circumstances – for "this is the will of the Lord for you". And not to "despise prophesying", that is to have ears to hear and to obey the Lord's daily word to us. Then the Holy Spirit will fill your life and His Spirit will make the fire of positive faith increasingly burn brighter.

No more going back to the "dark night of the soul". Praise God for His lifting power!

* * *

"I will praise thee, O Lord my God, with all my heart: and I will glorify thy name for evermore. For great is thy mercy toward me: and thou hast delivered my soul from the lowest hell" (Psa. 86:12–13).

3

THE WAY OUT

*This final chapter is the testimony of the Rev. W. E.
Leach, who was helped out of depression by this booklet
when it was first printed.*

It was during a time of depression that Mr.
Sparkes' booklet came into my hands soon after its
first publication. It is very often God's way to
provide various links in a chain to help a Christian
at a time of need: this booklet was one such link,
and as the author lived in the city where I resided at
that time I was able to thank him personally for
putting such practical, yet Biblical, advice on paper.
I am happy therefore to add a further word at the
conclusion of this revised edition by way of thanks.

When depression first overtook me I was completely baffled, and true to the experience outlined
in this booklet I felt far from God, and questioned
His will and the circumstances which helped to
bring about an accompanying sense of despair. I
felt as if I was in a world of my own and experienced
a deep sense of loneliness, unable to share the burden
even with close friends, though they must surely have
detected it! I had been a Christian for several
years, and had experienced much joy in serving the
Lord Jesus, and now this prolonged depression. Was

my Christian life real or imaginary? This I could answer. I had seen God at work miraculously in my life and the lives of others. I could not doubt that. Why didn't God lift the darkness when I prayed? He did, though not all at once. The vicious circle continued with all its unhappiness. The temptation to become morbidly introspective was very real, and it seemed that my days of Christian ministry were over. How could I ever preach and teach God's wonderful salvation again?

I realised that this was no ordinary feeling of depression which would go as quickly as it came. It lasted for many months. Looking back now I can see some of the causes that are easier to define at a distance. I had left the denomination in which I had been nurtured after deep heartsearching, and my future became uncertain, though I had been clear about God's call to the ministry. Deep feelings of failure ensued. Other problems arose of a personal and emotional nature and tensions mounted up. The biggest problem of all was the inability to combat by will-power the depression which came. It had a vice-like grip. The tendency was to believe that I was an isolated case. Loneliness makes one feel like that. Far from being the case I came to realise that there were and are numerous Christians facing the same kind of depression which sickens their mind, disharmonises the body, and agonises the soul. That is why this booklet is so relevant today. It will surely bring a little healing oil to troubled mental waters.

What were the steps towards deliverance? Before I outline these let me hasten to add that every day since has not been like an Indian summer. There have been dark days, but God in His love has helped me to see the cause and effect, and to know how to cope with signs of depression when they reappear. First, I had to recognise that the human mind is just as liable to sickness as the body. Mr. Sparkes makes this very clear. How well he brings out the essential differences in our personalities and make-up; this is all very helpful. Another step was to be prepared to talk over the problems with someone who would really understand and have professional help. This is not a shameful thing. It is really essential, because one is unable to share these feelings with just anyone. (Would all Christians really understand or even counsel one correctly.) It is important to be open and honest with God too, and to be prepared for Him to have His way. He teaches us submission and utter reliance upon Himself even when we may seem powerless to pray.

I could go on to say how the Holy Spirit has enabled me to see the resources that are in Christ, and to know His peace. After five years in another pastorate with all its problems and strains I have been able to counsel and pray with others whose lives have been overcome by depression and all sorts of difficulties.

God does deliver. He does come to our aid. May this booklet be used in His hands to be the means of strength and comfort to others who need its guidance.